HOLOGLYPHS

Twilight Fields

HOLOGLYPHS

Twilight Fields

S. K. Yeatts

First Edition

ISBN 13 978-1-945752-08-7

Cover art: S. K. Yeatts—*Le Sirenuse archipelago*

Holo   noun \hō-lə-\ or \hol\ whole; entire; complete

Glyph   noun \glif\ image or symbol that conveys
                 information nonverbally

Hologlyph   noun \hō-lə, glif\ whole image

Contents

HOLOGLYPHS

Twilight Fields

49 Days

White voices
Circle above the cathedral in snow and dark poppies of October.

Without end, an old evening returns.

Before winter,
A broken nimbus of moon burns in the Bardo's clear light.

Over a yellow harvest –
Flaming calendars of stars emerge,
Where luminous autumns cover tired hands in linen and rich frost.

It is only this after-image of finished candles –
A wild wind of providence,
And eternity passing like echoed-ghosts along the empty Zócalo.

A closing door.

Everywhere – night and the grand illusion.

Above Víznar
<Siguiriya para Federico>

Over long shadows of the garden,
A thin blood-line of morning –
A cross on the mountains of Sierra de la Alfaguara –
Far away, the purple trilling of one bird.

Without a confession, you follow a dead candle of moon,
Up through chalk balconies
          wound with orange capsicum and geraniums –
Past el Fuente Grande and ecru walls in voices of sleep —
Past the dark squares of Spain.

Over the consuming night,
Stars in red jasper anointed a collapsing shadow.
Everywhere, silver bones of katsura trees rustled:
A muffled arc of steps ending in the still olive grove.

White carnations rippled in the dark
          like a simple weave of burial linen –
Scepters of tall grass beat the air in rushing wings.
Far away, one bird pronounced your name.

In a night of falling camellias,
You will breathe cold air and taste nettles of lime.
You will kneel to a broken coda of guitars:
On the ridge,
A lunar wind will prance like a rider-less, chess-black horse.

Above Víznar, in the small hours,
A final image formed at your mouth:
Three girls with paper roses in the reddening esplanade:
A storm of bougainvillea and violet henna of dawn.

Beyond the summer, a rumor of messiahs will end.
A pieta of weeping acacias will bend
       across an empty field.
Myrrh of blank heavens will open –
A withered zodiac will circle your head in final landscape of poems.

Over long shadows of the garden,
A thin blood-line of morning –
A cross on the mountains of Sierra de la Alfaguara –

Far away, the faint pavane of one bird.

Aeolian Evening

At the end of summer,
Storms come unending from evening's closing tunnel:
The finished gold of the larch.

In dry light
Red figs ripen on unkempt lawns,
     where erosions of carved gods bend by a white bench.

Old stories haunt a space of the dream's minimal music.
Everywhere the glacial advance of evening:
A light of lavender and creeping thyme —
The full poppy's cry of passion —
An incense of oceans and pears —
The still radiance of the passing afternoon.

At the end of summer,
It is only to give up the dark silver herb of memory.
It is only to let go the accelerating day.

After August

After the hiss of mistral,
Pendulums of geese arc overhead in a slow white time.

Cicadas die down in the shadows of linen fields,
And silver steps of scythes deliver rosaries of frost on gold of cut hay.

After August,
Afternoons become remote in the wizened day.

The affairs of men are mostly empty.

Wolves and angels come down at evening
        to crumbling lamps of the village.
Stars and night curve around your silent face.

Artifact Ghost
<For L. J. Borges>

Evening streets end in a dried stain of bronze bells,
And cloud-shapes of τετραγράμματο.

By a cherry's weeping fountain,
Ghosts wait in the garden
Where remaining blossoms hold back a final cold of spring.

In the lunar courtyard –
Motets of wind become the prayers of god.

With faces in the mirror – not our own,
False histories of all worlds begin to fade.

All night,
Your lost voice –
And cries of the white-wing dove.

At Harvest

In unkempt grounds of afternoon –
Silence, and hesitations of light.

Water drips from a stone fountain carved of monks and pale satyrs.
Purple fruit comes out of a cistern of radiant autumn.

After our day,
A blue resonance of old worlds returns.

Jewels of sun linger without purpose on wet arbutus trees.
A wind starts at the narthex of long fields.
Almost, and always –
Urgent murmurs of golden grass sweep these empty hours.

In whispers, black grapes overcome a rusted fence,
And leaves spiral like ospreys over twilight fields.

At evening,
Our shadows stretch across these pale cobbles
Like numerals of a clock:
Footsteps pacing night's gravel.

Out of sleep's dark watermark,
Stars in flickered linens lean together like fallen arches of white stones.

After our day, old worlds of afternoon –
Silence, and hesitations of light.

Beauvoir

Golden blooming broom of moon
Sweeps a sleep of silver olives.

Over fallen fields,
Light years of lavender
Paint waves against crumbling cliffs of violet twilight.

Shadowed hands of poplars circle toward midnight
Under a clock face of silent stars.

Before Spring
<For Po Chü-I>

Before spring,
Golden light and shrouds of iron trees paint a long promenade.

Bergamot oil of moon
Scents a still courtyard of eroded stone angels.

Crows carry a last trace of the vesper bell further into night,
As stars burn in dead scriptures above the bowed head.

No one ever was.

Bellinzona
<At Vecchio>

Along the square,
Drowned faces ripple from marble urns –
At your feet, a road of a thousand stones begins.
Wrought-iron balconies and green shutters
        coil across this soft decay of Europe.

In expanding ripples,
Autumn's metastatic spread completes an old circle.

Out of earth's intangible spin,
Ghosts lean by flickered walls
        under exact disarray of stars.

Here - a troubled music returns in the dust of our ancestors.

Walking back,
Chrysanthemums and slow shadows descend in weathered light:
Twilight brims with dead voice of angels.

Overhead, scrawled notes of wild birds slant away in *accens plaintifs*:
A rustle of deserted worlds,
        and life's long moment.

When night arrives,
We drift along wet streets like wraiths of extinguished candles.

Beyond Light

At the hour of smoke,
Our silhouettes fall to fountains of poplars,
Tracing the steps to evening.

Beyond light,
Harvest fires repeat a pale rumor of worlds,
Where ghosts struggle in the black cathedral of their fathers.

Over the courtyard,
Choirs complete a dust of music –
Dim scripts of lamentation behind the sacred voice.

Everywhere,
Particles of light wave in a dark rain of autumn wheat.

By the village wall,
Arc of stars silver to a false compass.

In the Pi of non-repeating dreams,
Stained faces of carved youths' grace a stone gate.
Snow and doves descend from evening's troubled terrace.

Beyond light, only dusk's smooth decay.

Night and folded hands.

Blue Maria and the Insane Boy
<At the Mass of Grace>

In the streets,
A great debris of light brings stillness and algebra of faces.
An incomplete red of the wine –
Numbers without equation –
This irrational arch of evening.

Purple matracas rattle and spin before the votive mass.
Golden dust drifts in the streets like faint angels.

Painted scorpions and bright blood of carnations
            lamp the mercado.
At dark,
Cicadas sing an antiphonal liturgy.

From woven murals,
A mother and child linger by tumult of gardens –
Above them, the dead rock in an arid boat of deliverance.

Along the be-flowered esplanade,
Paper figures of Judas rise in flaming kites
            beyond circling shadows of children.

On a silver bench,
A priest is asleep with a book.

Fountains glimmer under a cranium of moon
Where bells wait in old towers like dark birds.

In the streets, an incomplete light –

He who is alone can only love humanity.

Calligraphy

Over the morning lake,
Crows spiral to spring storm of paper leaves.

In silk-prints,
Snow-clouds break into ten-thousand almond blossoms.

Chamonix

Our slow white summer
Fails in shadows of amber –

There, one autumn cloud.

Chant for the Feast of St. Ursula
<Te lucis ante terminum>

I.

City of evening
And blackbirds gather a lament for all this completed light.

On a path,
Pallid gardens open at your feet
In white grass of unfamiliar stars.

Roses fall in the dark for a dead savior.

II.

Seeded long ago,
Cold voices in polyphonic sleep
Wander through a residual red of plane trees.

At the edge of winter,
Bones of spiral heavens arch in soft elegies
On the counted stones of night.

Nothing will be as it was.
Everything has ended.

Come in from the light.

Chilpancingo

Coming back,
Red music drips from an old catalepsy of fountains –
A soaring darkness
and dead fire of purple Jacarandas.

In confused light,
Faces dissolve into exhausted Spanish arcades.
Groves of damp firethorns cover the shadows of women.

Nameless streets fill with dust and grackles.
Evening's white room closes.

Bells and wind drift over wild rye.
Erosions of murmured languages
          translate on a flickered wall.

Out of returning hours,
Autumn's fallen radiance.
Clocks shudder in a precise throb of hands –
And still urns of rainwater surround the empty plaza.

By the ward,
Patients wait in twilight courtyards
          like limp puppets.

In a flutter of old linens,
Doves of god ascend the whispered night.

Christmas in the Olives

<Evening Passio>

Christ in the olives
Brings a slow wound of dusk.
Clouds burn to doves and painted Icons of saints.

A dark Madonna gathers a failing light.

At the end of harvest,
A narthex of fields opens in purple and gold,
And mystery sonatas of winter fires
        complete a black Eucharist for the dead.

By a gate of red thorns,
Fountains drown carved shadows of angels.

From empty streets,
Bells paint circular hours -

And frost stains rosary windows
        with silver wreckage of stars.

Closing

Dusk's ruby light falls to incoherent evenings.

From upper rooms,
Dreamers hurl themselves into terrible distances.

In the square,
Lit water crumbles from excavated fountains –
All around, autumn's transubstantial red flows in the dying vein.

Walking wet streets,
Antique murmurs of the sleeping continue against the red light.

From twilight,
Wind pronounces white syllables of a dead name,
And a purple vapor of stars condenses to snow over the black grove.

The Savior is in exile –
The mountains passes are closing for the season.

Composite

Cypresses whisper in a red evening.
The entire year passes along cold streets
in snow and trembling lanterns.

There is a nightingale singing in black thorns of the Corsica tree.

Dry violets crumble into your hair,
Bringing night and stars.

Cornfields in Wind

Remaining fragments of the day.
Cornfields in wind.

At harvest,
We come down from eroded hills
        where black roses litter luminous autumns.

It is only this golden light passing over our bent shadows.

A decaying music of cathedrals lingers –
Angels in fallen architectures
Descend at the edge of rippling fields:
        pale statuary in smooth despair.

Always murmurs of wind tunneling behind twilight:
The antique voice of our fathers –
Slow whispers inside the distances
        of our few words.

It is only this golden light.

Remaining fragments of the day.
Cornfields in wind.

Crows at Evening

October returns in smoke of meadows:
        bush-clover and agrimony.
Hunters come back from a forest's drug of dusk:
        inlaid shadows circling empty hills.

Overhead,
Vermilion heavens whirl in syntax of darkness.
The wind's old opiate rustles an infinite language.

Startled by a deer's faint tremor,
A gust of crows shakes loose dark calligraphy:
        slow ink of wings on ricepaper skies –
        an apparition of poems beyond translation.

From genetic murmur of evening fields,
A cold wind turns the body to autumn.

I let golden coronas of leaves soar along the village road
As a drunken solider would release wild birds.

A temple bell counts an empty twilight of black heavens.

It is only to awake in the failing light that fills the momentary world.

Detached

A thousand doors close behind you,
As autumn mountains begin a red path.

How softly comes the fatal aria of the thrush.

Hours fall like leaves -
And on your lips,
A taste of roses beckons night.

From a breached perimeter of sleep,
Shadows gather in the betrayed garden.

Overhead,
A black quarantine of space
And stained zodiac of angels.

Dubrovnik

Byzantine light and dust of windows
Paints your still image.

In yellow wraiths of withered corn,
Autumn comes in the petrified song of the cuckoo —
And pendulums of waves on the grey sea-wall
Bring another evening.

Among blood and emerald of wild strawberries,
Shepherds wait under red-shifted constellations
In white years of original fire.

Somewhere,
Threnodies softly bleed from a dead choir.

From transfigured hours,
Saints crumble in cathedrals of abdicated light
And crows spiral in a vestment of vertigo skies.

All night,
Commemoration candles shiver in the dark.

Dusk

Clocks wind all the way back to the first word of the nightingale.
Around this terrace,
Dusk fills with grapes and sandalwood.

Out of this up-thrust light,
Rosettes of clouds ascend empty canals of early autumn skies.

As colors descend in sleep's wild glow,
Aster fields and the ancient cricket
Paint an ash of the distance between us.

Stone gates of the village close in golden debris of decayed bells.

Choirs die-away from a mezzotint of cathedrals,
And shadows over-run the empty garden in pink-noise of doves.

Always fountain-grasses at the end of summer
Waving in a white wind.

Over your folded hands, stars faintly rustle.

A thousand years of your silence continues to hold back the night.

Eikon III

Shadows climb the stones of Moustiers Sainte Marie all night.

By a crumbling wall,
Blossoms spread around a recalled evening.

An elegy of children
Runs in copper leaves of the ending summer.

From an eastern window,
The moon is a stone lantern.

Over this sad garden,
All our ghosts come back
Like perfect blue of empty skies.

Elysian
<Spukhafte Fernwirkangen>

Above the flooding night,
Voices like falling water recite names of the dead.

At the cathedral,
Blue pigment of storms covers peeling faces of saints
      with a rich impermanence of light.

At the hint of evening,
Crows watch for ghosts amid harvest's yellow rubble,
Where dark years tick from headstones' cloud-white hands.

Beyond rosary windows,
Streets are full of October and non-local color.

Transcriptions of feet count wet cobbles by an argument of fountains.

A glint of harvest scythes haunts the child's pale memory,
And runes of horses are startled by the sudden downpour.

Passing down through the days of the leaves,
Our shadows grow fainter and fainter at autumn's vacant gate.

Above the flooding night –
Sleep's tempest and brief soliloquy of stars.

It is only this impermanence of light,
      and whispered names of the dead.

End of Summer

Gold and silk of exiled skies continue.

Voices become a wind of fountain grass and poppies,
Where dusk's yellow score fills the larch with marcato of crows.

Out of this ending light,
Rosettes of cut-clouds float like coming blossoms of snow
        over ivory lines of ocean.

The gates of the village close in a passage of bells,
As the ancient chaconne of the cricket becomes still.

Your leaving
Completes a silence of ending worlds.

Stars rustle in faint Misereres over your grave all night –
Like remaining heat of stones after the summer has gone.

Entangled

Ice returns in aquamarine of entangled winter.

It is a bloodmoon and cut-wrist of cathedral bells –
Familiar shadows capturing some remaining light.

All our words embed in these autumnal stones,
With whispers of falling water and bright lament of birds.

It is circling chants of wind all night in remote fields
Filling the days of childhood with harvest's red hour.

Tonight,
Lamps are not lit for the living,
But for processions of the perfumed dead –
And we walk out again to where we begin.

Entangled –
Fragile histories cross the flooding Night
In a pale boat of preserved stars.

Evening Canvas

Brushes of blue ink
Paint a faint dusk of still hills:
Pale autumn iris.

Faint Angels at Agile

A thinning light in yellow streets.

At dusk,
Old fountains bring mirrored vineyards
over autumn's pale decline.

In gold wind of dying rye,
Bells tangle above dark histories.

A great music arcs over our little time.

Tonight, frost descends against the red grape.

Final Night in Venice

<At Isola di San Michele – for Ezra >

Darkness before evening,
And old blasphemy of storms comes over the Grand Canal
      completing your remaining days.

Out of time –
Flickered apparitions walk narrow streets in rain's rustling feet,
Delivering a city of shadows.

Carnival masques of smoke and stars
Expand to mystery above an empty piazza,
      erasing an imagined history.

Premonitions of the moment will fade.
You will be dust slipping through the fingers of dead suns -
Architectures of Istrian stone and ruins of light
      at the end of a long afternoon.

Not remembered,
Rocking on night's recurring wave,
You sleep in the black gondola of Venice until morning –

Until the end of the world.

Fire at Malahat Highlands

Poems go uncarved in passing frescos of clouds.
Dialogs of the sages are lost in the conscious observation.

All day –
Empty mountains fill with mist and ash of dragons:
A dark enigma-gate and light of the many worlds.

All night –
I wait on river stones,
Watching distant fires stalk the thin black line
        between earth and heaven.

 Who knows if we will arrive at the wilderness-gate of morning?

Torchiers of stars and the red grape
Continue to burn into the third watch.

For Georg

Over Galicia,
Eagles crumple about the dark cloth of your brow.
In the bloodstream: winter's white poem.

Constellations swarm to drugged nimbus above a weary god.

From the ash grove,
Night beckons the innocent.
With a siren voice,
Your unborn child delivers
        an empty heaven's terrible mirror.

A father walks with his young son
Where herds linger in blue and gold.
At evening, a heavy rain of cold stars.

Let the life drain from you —
Let the color run out from the violet hills — Sleep.

In the remnant of ruined garden,
All has long been accomplished.

For the Exile

From another dawn,
Jewels of dew light the universe.

In the valley below,
Crystals of finished suns
Set flame to a morning of village bells.

By a painted box of violets,
A girl in white is singing Wagner.
An oriel covers the highest notes without any score.

For this,
I have come back along the path of night and smoke.

From Pontikonisi

In the purple hour,
Lavender fields and the hot grey's of Crete
Draw a chorus of Aeolian harps from Mikonos to Thira.

Your cloud-white hair flies like Martins in a blue Aegean wind.
Lanterns swing in flickered marble and bone of olive-tinted fire.

In the courtyard,
All our words grow silent –
And a simple fountain pushes back the open robes of night.

Fuente Grande

Across a small space of black heavens,
Dancers come in a Soleá of extinguished candles.

Carnations litter the spring in a thousand years of moonlight,
Bringing only infinite worlds and a single empty night.

Awake to voices of wind
        and anguished face of carved angels –
Overhead, a fading mantilla of white stars . . .

And eventually, morning.

Funeral
<For Lee>

A north wind blows red and purple at the end of autumn.

Wine-lights of dusk
Course in drugged vein of leaves.

Beyond August,
You said *"half our lives are over,"*
And it was good . . .

Now, garnet processions of hills
Crowd around a silvered silk of morning,
And smoldered pyres of stars in recitatives
        of your ash and light.

Water does not carve a history through old rock.
Water and rock are mostly reflections of each other's stillness.

Seasons only spin in the pale moment,
Where all are neither here, nor not-here —
Without future or past — runes of old stars burning out forever.

At your funeral,
In the flickered cold of the gathered afternoon,
I knew you were no more (*nor no less*) present
Than any of the rest of us.

Fyrlykt
<Pharos>

In spinning fires of autumn —
A shelter of storms comes over the next hill.

From the coast,
Lightning finds a momentary shore —
        calling out with no reply,
Where old beacons of stars burn in slow circles.

This house will fall.

Ships at the song of siren-oceans
Run aground on night's reef of angels —
And black rocks cradle a silver wave of the drowned voice.

Under compass of gulls,
Searching all these darkening skies,
A long vigil begins.

This house will fall.
Ash of seaweed will wrap pale arms,
And twilight's wet fire will bloom in your onyx hair.

Ghost Bells

At dark,
Echoes of past voices embed in deep fields of snow.

From our silver hours,
Bells drift to ghosts in a finished clockwork of stars.

Night closes around some finite circling years
In frost and stillness of a completed eternity.

Focus becomes lost in the doppelgangers of now.

It is only some small point between the inhale and exhale –
Between reflections of shadow and fire.

Procul recedant somnia et noctium phantasmata

At dark,
We have never been here.
No one is observing.
There are no bells.

Greve

Summer falls to chrysanthemums of a failing sun.

Closer to now,
Last days circle in blue and gold stillness
        among the gardens of Castello di Uzanno.

A frost of olive trees,
Weathers to patinas of storms and swollen fruit.

From a garden of wind,
Approaching forms of passing light
Wake near-human statuary of cypress and dark poplars.

Evening's wooden gate closes.

Above the village,
Monochromes of startled sculptures
        litter the night with broken marble of stars.

Fashioned on nothing,
We are ghosts of ghosts –
Our footsteps ticking like pendulums of clocks
Against darkening garden paths toward morning.

Homeland

<For Nelson Stokes>

You walk into ocean,
       among burned-out lamps of October –
A drowned chorus,
And brush-strokes of unfinished red seasons.

From fragmental hours,
All light drifts away from the eye's vacant mirror.
In a pendulum of waves,
The moon arcs toward midnight over our empty hands.

At dark,
Near-human shadows wash ashore
       against a final erection of stars:
Nimbus of seaweed gracing fallen faces.

On returning to the homeland,
The world breaks into golden light –
But hearing only pounding of the charcoal autumn,
You close up your evenings,
And walk into ocean.

In a Garden

Night trails clouds in shard of souls.

My heart has begun to deteriorate,
And leaves of my fingers clutch black wind and writhe.

Walking back,
A Latin Canon of crows traces the narthex of the ear,
And warped faces ripple up from a tarn of empty streets,

Over cassocks of storms,
Burial linens of stars curl above the momentary rustle of man
In the unpronounceable names of god.

In a garden,
I dimly note your shrouded figure
Like an urn holding a final wreckage of dreams:
A nimbus of thorns for this fallen house . . .

I come for you in the hour's slipping fire –
A discord before winter -
A non-local shadow
        circling in a coma of certain steps.

Night trails clouds in shard of souls.

It is a forgiven Eucharist of red light and stones –
An exhausted kiss for the master.

In the Afternoon

Fruit and angels decay beyond open doors –
A peripheral blur of completed lives.

Darkness is spoken in the stillness of your summer room.

Over affannoso of fountains,
Embalmed stars rock in night's sunken boat.

Black oaks form shadows of clock-hands on a carved gate.

In perfect ruins of afternoon light –
A drone of doves calls the hours
From crumbling church towers.

Ingeborg

A black breath of wind goes before you.
At your back,
Bare trees bend over the pale avenues of men.

Death is the chosen one,
As skies fill with an after-glow of the ashen voice.

Over many nights, we sit quietly in this house of storms.
All summer long – the words do not come,
Where drown statues wait all night
        in the empty piazzas of Rome.

Overhead –
Madrigals of completed stars burn out,
And fountains paint white noise of poems
        from *Il Giardino delle Cascate*.

Ash is light – Nothing is lost.

La Colonia

Beyond the stain of water dripping over stone – the day calls no name.

Waves of wind in olives line the morning
In antiphonal chant.

At the end of August,
You came in flickered fire of clearing streets
Like captured voices of the dead.

Ending moonlight
And years slip away at the edge of the hand
        in a final scent of clematis.

Carved light of morning will circle an old infinity.
Multiple lives will always be lost.

From La Colonia –
An end at the beginning,
Where it is more than these pale angels of first light –
More than kneeling skies hardening to white wings of dawn –
More than funeral torches
        burning on the mountains of Sierra de la Alfaguara.

You are cypress, sandalwood and dark linen.
You are whispered rivers and faint song of the dove.

Beyond the stain of water dripping over stone – the day calls no name.

In murmured absolution of Fuente Grande,
Everything is forgiven.

Leaves

The evening returns in dark linen.

At the mouth of still seasons,
Bells tick away an autumn half-life.
Archangels huddle about a purple gash of heavens.

Across the courtyard,
Silver motets climax from black cathedrals.
A dead frost of leaves haunts the days of man.

Listen - they are falling at the edge of the porch.
They are falling into the deep cut of twilight,
Filling long October fields –
Crimson-gold drug of remembrance and decline.

From the open window,
Oil-lamp forests wait in night's legend.

It is only the old prisms of the leaves
Floating in glittered wreckage about the fallen garden.

The evening returns –
Bright histories blowing away
Through the long flicker of the world.

Li Po in Spring

T'ang light:
Weak wine – Strong blossoms.

For the exile,
Hesian cherries weep in a pinkwind.

Dividing infinity,
Clouds come in carvings of poems:
Petals of white bells under Orion's cold bloom.

All night,
Cranes float like shadows of dragons,
And a wind at Sanzu temple repeats your name.

From black bamboos of Tanzu mountain,
Falling rocks become faint thunder in a paused wind.

So few evenings go to make up a season,
Where even the emperor cannot bring back a single fallen flower.

For you,
It was enough to dream in remote jade fields,
And let the world slip away.

Lines at Caux

Shadows of autumn and straw-flowers.

Summer goes out in bright streams of fish—
Afternoons collapse like the fading
        strength of our hands.

Beyond the portico,
An after-glow arrives on night's blue hill.

A peripheral motion of moon returns at the close of your life.

Silent statues wait in the courtyard.
Everywhere,
Sparrows flutter to luminous angels of decayed light.

How troubled and perfect are all that have lived.

Lotus

A flickered narthex of olive hills
Brings dark fruit of autumn.

After this heat,
A still garden harbors some faint motion of ghosts,
Where blue wind of twilight holds a cold urn of stars.

On an overgrown path,
You walk in white-noise of flowers
        under scrawled expansion of storms.

All night,
A glitter of lotus leaves drifts in jade's pale fire
As stepping stones for the dead

Magician

In the malachite storm,
A disturbing relief of dreams.

Beyond the raised hands,
Men become more effective as ghosts.

Metaphors spring with convincing passion
From the decomposing mouth.

Shadows of shadows,
Whose dry voices god could not understand.

At the purple hour,
Crumbling angels hesitate
By the edge of golden larch groves.

Along the vacant square,
No one is coming.

Poem by poem, the heart ticks into obscurity.

Magnum Mysterium
<sobria ebrietas>

I.

Consciousness runs out through the gaps in the world like water.

On silvered nights, heat of prayer escapes
      into frozen heavens.
In a slow dervish,
Recurring constellations
Loom back over our same hours.

Doves in dark arias ascend beyond a white vestment of streets.

Along the piazza,
Luminous robes of snow
      and monastery choir's echoed magnificat —
Everywhere, black crosiers of trees
      fill with wind's cold alcohol.

In blue fields,
The dead fill the night like geodes.

II.

Poets hemorrhage in a dead astronomy of their forefathers.

On the verge of meaning,
Our shadows stretch across the pale-rose stones
Like numerals of a clock.

III.

A Margaux glow in the red wound of evening.
Unfiltered light of the moment comes back against short seasons.

Evolving out of sleep into open acres,
I have sensed my shadow at the forested edge of dreams:
A white stillness at the rim of eternity.

Above the ragged garden,
Deep constellations' forbidden fruit
        overwhelm the rumored embolus of soul.

It is not you or I in the world's dwindling color:
We are legion –
The light is everywhere.

Minerva

<"Error is all in the not done">

— Pound

A deterioration of unpracticed hands —

Poets with a cortege of twilight hours
Prowl the ruined city like autumn.
In forbidden drug of color,
Praise smolders from black temples
        delivering melismatic nights.

Always,
Blood-tint leaves pound back under breathless heavens
And stars loom to burned calendars
        and silver rubble of god.

At evening's great indigo,
An owl in dim branches soars at the remnant of light.
There is nothing to be done.

Momentary Stillness of Empty Color
<For Lorca >

A light of your hands fills this shadowed garden
With olive blossoms and red jasper of grapes.

With ivory birds of morning –
From far fields,
You hear the cricket of death –

But it sings.

Neimand bleibt hier

On the crest of night,
Clouds leave in white shards of souls.
Taurus will not stand in the way.

Entangled with evening,
At last sun,
You wait in a shadowed door.

In counted stars,
The sound of a bell
That will not arrive for thousands of years
Completes a still garden.

After summer's silhouette and jade pitch,
Eternities of worn light come over empty fields
         in voices of the dead.

Timeless,
Photons whirl in the closing wings of an iris.

Out of this impermanence:
Old circles of fire –
A gesture of moments –
A clock's non-local shadow,
And bright scalene patterns of stars
         trace our imagined worlds.

On the crest of night,
Clouds leave in white shards of souls.

No one will remain.

Nepenthe

Under evening's violet soma,
A last defense of chrysanthemums floods the still battlefield.
White and gold pennons flame over the buried ivory bone.

Circling the village,
Dusk goes out in alter-candles of tossed linen fields.

Short seasons collapse in a silver cremation of the living.

Grazing herds wander in confused light,
Where a rough wind blows crumbling stars into black eternities.

Among empty hills,
You climb on dark clocks of sleep —
Everywhere, a background-radiation of winter
        with returning calendars of ash.

Again - a familiar sequence of days ends.

I have come for you,
Only to find ruined moonlight,
        and a long finished dust of music.

Night at Fussen
<Vox Inamis Caelum>

Twelve bells circle an empty heaven.

In pale shadows,
Sparrows rise above the crumbling gold of men.

On the forest path,
We came upon embers of stars,
And silver crucifix of Katsura trees.

From remaining stones of the church,
Peeling eyes of saints stare from dead histories.

Under rustling lamentation of falling water,
Russian olive trees become a black wind.

The same bird sings.
Already it is dark.

Autumn's still wilderness follows.

Night Snow – Black Stones

Pale sirens at the end of the year
Come in night snow and a sky of black stones.

The path to the monastery was littered with ghosts
        and vast forests of trackless moss –
Islands of storms embedded in raked sand.

All these dark winds circle like wolves
Back in a perfect ruin of mountains:
Stone faces in gothic arches
        and pale sculptures of petrified saints.

Torches of December burn out.
Motets of the whippoorwill echo distant matins all night.

Non Local

Spent vineyards deliver harvest's immaculate decay.

Old roses and Chinese firs
Entangle to soliloquies of night.
Suspended color fades at the back of the mind.

Below evening's balustrade,
A passing red of gardens emerge.
Flickered walls and shadows of clematis
Overrun autumn's deserted barricade.

It is an architecture of the tomb's yellow grain
That comes to your door in the night:
Fallen florets of dusk's ergot light
        and the moon's indole ring.

By a parterre, in altered light,
Carved faces sing from a white fountain.

On silver air,
Voices of old trees enter a still room.
Arabesques of ripe olives do, and do not, fall.

At the close of youth,
Hymns rise from dust of lips,
and fire dims on the heavy grape.

        In the gradual and step by step descent,
From a clock's shroud,
Black labyrinths of hands grope slipping hours.

Frost comes across locked shrines of a cloned day,
Where a thousand years fall away
        in the same moment.

Unobserved –
Out of the beginning
Out of the great twilight of worlds
Out of the distances of one –

Never together – Never apart:
Nothing ever was anyway.

Notre-Dame de Sénanque Abbey

From the terrace of morning,
Birds spin a simple silk
And rosary of aerial prayers:
Ink-strokes of worship stitching this lilac shroud of Provence.

Chants of water over stone —
Chants of cicadas in roses —
Chants of wind through robes of the olive
Bring a Passio of old light.

At the end of spring,
As the rains grow quiet,
Even a closed window
        cannot keep back fallen ghosts of cherry-flowers.

With all these lost blossoms,
Only the moon remains along dark branches
        in scattered fire of seeds, light and memory.

Oaxaca

<Dia de los Muertos>

From white arcades and glitter of graves,
Skulls and marigolds form altars in the dark.

By the cathedral,
It is only a flight of paper ghosts,
Where children with bone-colored kites run against a pale wind.

Drifting toward midnight,
The Moon's belladonna feeds mute colors of lament,
        with scattered eulogies of autumn doves.

Coming out to music of circling streets,
Plagiarized dreams and mezcal of bells
Wash past your face in scent of fruit and agave.

In drowned silhouettes,
Young girls bring flowered devils, bread and small apples of dawn.

At the end of the old world,
Along a river of dancers,
We come carrying baskets of fire,
        as failed gods to a forbidden land.

Skeletons hang in the trees,
And corn leaves wreath the bowed head of the savior
        with bright masques of lace and ash.

Across the candled cloisters of Mexico,
Eternity is written in sand -
Torches paint an old robe of memory –

And the living continue to sleep with the dead.

On the Border

Yellow maize of bells calls twilight down through a red autumn.

Scroll paintings of falling water hang at the end of the world,
As empty cruets of stars advance in white ink of birds.

Over your grave,
A branch of September-olives kneels in silver lace,
        and night opens pale robes of wind.

Ancient seas of withered corn whisper from golden hours
Beneath Sistine skies.

At dusk,
Voices become still.
A purple wine of hills harden to diamond-ash of a first snow.

Blackbirds wait in crumbling shadows of dark monuments:

The last sleep of the innocence.

Past Grace

A sonata of wild birds
Releases a flight of winter bells.

Dark hands of lovers
Writhe like storms under entangled sheets of skies.

All night,
Stars pass over a chance of lost worlds.

In the catalepsy of waking,
Silver herbs of winter bring a distant morning.

Gliding past grace,
From the remains of too many lives,
A forgiving light is blocked.

At the end of radiance:
Your perfect face.

Recitativo

Time past comes again
To time future –
Which is no time.

It was going to snow,
And I watched the lights end like commemoration candles
       and a held breath of shadows.

Chorales of wind wound around stone angels,
And cries of the white-wing dove:
Choruses like falling ice before morning –
But we were already asleep.

I could repeat your name,
But it would become no clearer,
And these streets would be as empty.

Over our luminous silhouettes,
Past and future merge:
Moon and star imprinting a calm exhale of mistral.

In no time,
It was going to snow –
We were asleep,
And I waited for the whisper of your name.

Reply for Juan Ramón Jiménez

It was still when I saw you in the garden at nightfall –
A beggar in an art of stones –
A silhouette of god.

When did you arrive?
I recall the end of the afternoon
        and a gloom of empty streets.
It was a shadow of hydrangeas that drooped like a sleeping man.

A silver hand at the open window. –
(*or was it closed*?)
Did you speak, or was it some pale octave of leaves?
It was windy – our hair was black and the night was gray.

By the clock,
The window was closed. –
(*or was it open*?)
I crouched in the garden at nightfall:
A sleep of toppled stones...

When did I leave?
It was a shadow of hydrangeas that you saw –
No beggar in the empty streets –
No silhouette of god –

Only a black night,
Only silver hands and gray hair
In the stillness of the afternoon.

Roma Streetscape: October

A rust of dusk follows young girls over swollen grey cobbles,
Where iron bells and a failing Brunello sun
Paint the Piazza del Popolo with early autumn.

The same evening comes again.

I know you have given up this world.

Saeta

Regard the white bush of ghosts,
And how your life runs out like shadows at evening.

Over bronze ruin of wheat,
Debris of starlight arcs back in the dark skull -
     still years of light circling a timeless room.

By the black canal,
Your face flickers to October and a broken light of saints.

Outside:
The winter night's old phosphor
Brings a siren of wolves in frost's armory —
They loom at the edge of dead fields:
On the tip of the tongue.

Along a cry of vacant streets,
In reflected cobbled faces,
Only a white interior of passing years
     and slow pendulum of feet follow.

Silver is the lunar clutch of the poplar.
In ending cadence, wind, like leaf-fingers on guitars
Drifts above the dim village in smoking ash of forfeit heavens.

Colors are drunk with monochrome.

The dance will end.
Fountains lament all night in the empty square.

Sainte-Chapelle

Unborn
Eternal morning.

Cut-glass of cobalt skies
Ascend over our little time.

Red and blue-shifted heavens
Arc beyond delivered histories.

Expanding worlds circle in clocks of fire,
Where fixed light of multiple lives stain this bright sleep.

Released forever,
Infinite colors bring sounding octaves and a ghost of the only moment.

Clouds of vast choirs return —
We come forward:

Oratorios of silence, light and forgiveness.

Sashuis

Light sways over dusk bridges in shadow of horses.

Golden octave of composers floods narrow streets.

In a long-dried violence of color,
Evening's old suicide
Hangs back in locked museums.

Above the Béguinage,
Through crooked relic of willows –
Stars slowly lose synchronicity.

Dark waves return along the coast,
As bells and terns count a falling circle of hours.

Black oceans wash away even time's finest agates.

Satori

Stars bloom in luminous arcs.
Time unwinds along the autumn nerve.

In a garden,
Statues of Chinese warriors rise from the snowy clearing:
Lit fountains of stone meeting all commitments.

On the returning path,
A single rhododendron's white galaxy unfolds.

You will die in no country.
You will recall the scent of the night.

Seven Grasses of Autumn

Among seven grasses of autumn:
Gutei holds up one finger.
A bird sings.
Ancient light rustles from green torches of cryptomeria.
Crows fly for hours.
Water pours from the upper lakes all night.

Out of sleep, a dark universe ripens.

At the close of the ninth month,
A great wind arrives in ghostdance
          of untroubled leaves.

I should abandon public life
While the color yet remains.

Siguiriya

Behind flickered facades,
Fingers of guitars bring shadows to the corners of flame-painted rooms.

Dry flowers embalm the pear of fall
In torch-light of a full moon.

A black horse comes up an empty street.

Old light bleeds in mercury from a distant wail of stars,
And a dance of voices circles your head in aural fire.

Calendars expire.
A rich patina of youth ends.

Everywhere, night mounts its yellow assault.

Silent Evening

As fields become dark with returning spring –
It will be a decayed pear in the wooden bowl of night,
And flowing sargenes of twilight that hide your face.

It will be blue pools reflecting
Stone statues aching for a passing life.

It will be echoes of angel-ravaged architectures
And recitatives of fountains all night.

It will be dark matins spilling from the golden hemorrhage of evening,
And the camellia's red frequency.

It will be a triptych of cathedrals,
Rising in clasped hands beyond the reach of men.

It will be the burnished cherry's brief hail of passion,
And a soft ruin of Europe
        rippling to lost faces in the blackness at your feet.

It will be before we leave –
Where nothing can be changed,
As fields become dark with returning spring.

Simulation II

In slowing circles of the repeated day,
A Stellar Jay paints shadows over our autumn house.

For hours,
Clouds come in tendrils of mint and black anise.

On the next hill,
I sense your long sleep.

In valerian and purple vinca,
A wind becomes still –
The long count of the held breath.

It was enough to notice growing shadows out in the garden –
Enough to sense the recursive aria of an unfamiliar bird -

And perhaps it was just the repeated day –
Only the spiraling of a Stellar Jay over our autumn house –

Or not.

Snow at Evening

Cold angels descend around night's stone wall —
Stars dwindle in serpents of light.

Above a coma of whispered fountains,
White worlds expand over our silver decline.

We come back through a faint snow at evening
        under thin smoke of prayer —

In pale alarms,
Our feet tick on black cobbles
Like hungry ghosts counting the steps to eternity.

Soglio

I.

As we sleep –
Beyond the year's glacial advance,
Ochre heat and the sun's flowering lemon at noon.

Over haunted seasons,
Oleanders litter stone streets of your desire.

From chords of the falling day and evening's red cup,
Aural landscapes drift like a white violence of clouds.

In the moment's faint coma of color,
Scent of lavender quiets a dark octave of clocks.
Behind you, your hands reach from a mirror's blue stillness.
Night is spilled against a withered mantle of angels.

From open crypts of moonlight,
Roses stain the hands of the dead.

II.

As we sleep –
Stone pines and whirling cypresses sweep extended skies.
Storms fountain over Italy's cerulean pools,
Where young girls come back across white esplanades
        with braids of dusk in their hair.

In lunar prayers,
Hooded clerestory of hills arises at evening:
        as a ritual on whispered lips.

In the gathered dark,
A passing glow of sacramental grapes
		swell in the veins of the fallen.

Moments in time
Erode a completed future and blooming tumult of stars.

III.

As we sleep —
Amber afternoons of wind cover us in old light.
Between the wars,
Bronze temples of wheat stretch before and after.

Autumn continues over
A golden string-theory of vineyards.

Around our histories —
Fissures of night open over our empty hands.

From a perfect confusion,
Ghosts kneel by smoldered shadows of the living —
Urns of remembrance,
Bringing evening's pale score, and the passing voice.

Everywhere, a sacred luminescence fades.

It is only twilight coming again to the edge of your face,
As we sleep.

Soleá

Hills of autumnal fires and sorrow.

Oil lamps drain a light of leaves
And immense darkness in the olive grove.

Small girls in seda shirts
Kneel at the altar of a wooden Christ.

Dogs argue in echo of narrow streets.

A wind of guitars and faded carnations
Pour out into the purple evening
of your death.

Sorrel River

Worn cliffs and falling leaves
Calm a short history:
This blue fountain of autumn.

By the river,
Yellow candles of poplars
Bring back spent evenings
      in a parchment of twilight fields.

When Orion comes up in a silver skiff of fire,
Our voices ink aural shadows along the village wall—
And we go so slowly.

Over the stone towers of men,
The dark sky is brushed with sparrows
As silk threads of moonlight
Spin clouds from your still white hair.

Spanish Steps

Doves bring morning in aural greys and ivory.
Dawn clouds blossom over the broken fire of Rome.

Bougainvillea and white ash of fountains
Calm summer's still lemon.

At Santa Maria della Concezione,
Wet coins of camellias cover bright eyes of the dead.

With sound of feet over song-worn steps,
Oleanders and terracotta winds surround your fertile sleep.

Spring Snowfall

In spring's slow canto,
Blossoms litter a red-shift of floating fields.

Copper fire of lanterns
Swing in black verses at the ferry crossing,
Where boats return in a thousand waves of cold chrysanthemums.

Over folded hands,
White birds blow to origami of roses over a drained pool.

Past dreams,
I awake to accidental remainders of stars,
        arcing over the last bridge of night.

It is only a short confusion.

Stalker on Temple Mountain

I.

It will snow.
A shadow will come along the closed mountain pass -
It will be the last singing bird of night.

At twilight,
Silhouettes of temples crumble in pale choirs.
Everywhere,
Talismans of yellow leaves cannot stop the evening.

It will begin where it ends:
Shadows of shadows –
The mangled voice of god –
Speech of old oceans
        climbing dark rocks all night.

At the stained window,
Something like an owl flickers across a closed eye of moon.

In returning histories – mercury falls.
The house is locked in sleep.
It will snow.

II.

Three hundred seasons expire in the clear light of sparrows.

III.

In the moment before is the moment after.

Shadow and object –
Echo and voice.
A long elation brings remains of aging afternoons,
        where ruined pears paint an autumn table.

Above us,
Stars close over the village gate in sopranos of wind.
Tibetan singing-bowls fill a garden's pentimento.

Ghosts leave in silence and guilt,
As old light becomes permanently embedded
        in a stone walls of uncompleted lives.

Unwound shadows of a clock
Approach a perimeter of night
        on slowing silver hands of the coming hour.

Out of time –
Something back in the cold of mountains
        not like living men begins moving toward dawn.

It will snow.

Shadow and object -
The last singing bird of night.

Star at St. Remy

Blossom of fire –
Bold stroke of cold zinc,
      holding course in ultramarine seas.

Final notes of the viola da gamba
      and night's coda softly begin.

From open windows,
Flowers of flame over the garden's white sleep slowly ascend –
Aerial rose – bird of light:

Always –
This one silence and clarity before the old horns of morning.

Still Return

Quiet autumn comes in with dark music.

A golden drug of evening bells
       extinguishes a red field.
Everywhere, a rich light recedes.

Courtyards of grapes and fountain grass emerge.
Statues in the empty grove lament for distant worlds.
Crows clot at night's still return.

Our voices echo into seasons of recurring grain:
       dry wind in sullen plumes of wheat –
       yellow maize of constellations:
       a last light loose above the world.

In fleury of churches,
Christ kneels in a cut-glass wilderness -
A flickered stain of doves circling the bowed head.

Crickets pulse faint anthems,
And clouds writhe overhead in purple calcination of angels:
The long storm of the soul.

Saints stagger in drunken halo of streetlamps –
Fountains, sorrel, and torch-light stars deliver a pale memory.

Along blue alleys, a rustle of dead color dies down.

Mystery returns in a flat-line of hours,
And for a moment,
An aster of moon lingers over the white boulevard,
Soothing the fallen verdure of the world.

Stillness at Kasha-Katuwe

Horizons of grey wind
Fill a redacted world.

December fires of piñon and cedar
Bring eroded choirs of night.

On the way,
An empty wash of stones became mica of stars.

Canyons of slate skies
Release columns of white bells.

Pale gatherings of vacant light
Come in footsteps of a failed path.

One thousand years pass.
Our luminous details begin to fade.

The ever-approaching moment
Is out on the dark chaparral.

Summer Fragment

Like Wang Wei –
With time, I become lazy about writing poems,
And let crows against an evening storm paint them for me.

Sunken Garden

Circles of rain fossilize on the lake.
Somewhere,
Stone wind chisels back in black calligraphy of bamboo.
Hidden rhododendrons
        wait for dawn's old red shadows.

In a long night –
Fires fades out.
A nightingale sings in the pale flower of my skull.

It was a thousand years ago.

The Guest

After the ghosts of evening have left the garden –
After the bells of the basilica fade –
After the blue fire of youth rises to yellow ash of stars–
Comes the guest.

Between the speech and speaking –
Between the dream and dreaming –
Between before and after –
Comes the guest.

Before the circle of all lives –
Before illusions of afternoon –
Before winter's silver vesper of frost –
Comes the guest.

Make ready the table and the lamps:
It is already snowing on a black robe of roads.
It is wind arriving in a wood-smoke of night.
It is the faint knock at the locked door.

Now is what has always been, and may yet be.

After the ghosts of evening have left the garden –
After your season of old age –
After the dead reckoning of the moment –
Comes the guest.

Thunder at Montecatini Alto

From the castello,
A clock portends no time.

Under thin robe of clouds,
Light goes out below Montecatini Alto
Where olive trees walk up from the valley
        in a sliver raiment of sleeping saints.

By the Parco delle Terme,
Grey streets worn with feet of the dead
        cool a long afternoon.

Over stained rosary windows,
Faint homilies of thunder begin
        calming a field of wild strawberries.

Here –
At the terrace of ending worlds,
Stone angels hold trumpets of eternity –
And we wait with them,
As if there was something we could do.

Tofino

Night comes back on black watch of lost sailors,
Where glaucoma of lighthouses fail:
An ocean's deep urn, washing up recurring seaweed of stars.

Golden light dies back in cathedrals of old forests
Releasing the deaf choir of the sparrow.

Smoke ends the day in a cantus of wind and prayer.

With the autumn not yet come,
Red leaves of the soul already fall about these canyons
In impossible shadows.

Twelve Houses · Twelve Hours

One evening bell fades to many.

Before winter,
Dark angels appear along distant shadows of stone walls.

Solemn stars silence the year's-end,
And obelisks of cypress ascend to architectures of the spent day.

Without translation,
In an ash of hours,
Black calligraphy hangs on the passing wings of crows,
        where we have accomplished nothing.

Circling the cerulean pool of the eye,
Night comes up through grey olive groves like a hungry ghost.

Valle d'Aosta

With evening,
Weathered flags dance above dissolving countries –
In the square,
Our little darkness, and the wreckage of the day.

At the end of legends,
A remaining light of gods drowns in white speech of fountains.

From the cathedral,
Voices of wind score a pale chaconne
Where angels of dusk begin a long descent.

Without warning,
Shadows arrive at night's jade hill.

In the square - our little darkness.

Purple-grays of September are out in the garden allée.
Lanterns of chrysanthemums swing in the failing light.

Wet Streets and Roses: Michigan Avenue

Before the downpour,
Two violists play Mozart's D minor Romanza for tips.

Sparse crowds become a white noise of the bygone summer.

At twilight,
Ghosts arrive in rain and carvings of wind.

Over darkened canyons of the city,
Memory falls like rose petals from amber streetlamps.

Ever watchful,
Stone lions sleep all night on Michigan Avenue.

Whispers at the End of Summer

Gray doves in Bordeaux-light end the day.
Out of time,
In the circling dark,
Drown gods stare back from erosions of old fountains

Fallen leaves move in old gardens,
And darkness comes over the next hill.

Vineyards ascend to purple histories.

In whispers at the end of summer,
A single leaf falls forever onto a wrought-iron bench.

Long dead –
The living prepare for sleep.

White

So many crows flying over the western mountains,
I cannot sleep.

Shadows of waves lodge in the autumn willows.

Sleet falls on a river smoldered with
  coals of maple leaves.

By morning,
A new snow has frozen wild red thistles
  to a pure bolt of monochrome silk.

Xoxocotlan
<All Saint's Eve>

Black pottery of night forms over the Zócalo.
Bitter lime and milk-jade pools
     cool the brows of the dead.

A shroud of the Virgin waits
     in candled cathedrals.
Over dirt streets, an extinguished gold of the thrush.

At evening's woven sun,
Marigolds wreath forgotten gods –
Everywhere,
Pepper and cork trees sway.
     in a murmur of lanterns and passing crowds.

Winds in a scent of camphor follow through apparitions of dry corn:
A lost voice and shadows of carved angels.

Returning autumn spreads a spasm of red ecstasy,
Where distant husk of villages falls silent.

In an end of days,
Confused stars arc over a small harvest.

From a faint lamplight against your face:
The living are the dead.

Your Heaven is a Dark Evening

Your heaven is a dark evening
Filled with white plane trees and falling water.

Dirt streets empty into pale carnations of light,
And named-stones drain shadows from the cathedral.

A wind goes ahead of us in marionettes
Woven of the moon's dry leaves.

Thunder over the plaza brings birds of camellia petals
With hollow voices,
Speaking the names of god.

In a wrong tIme,
Unfamiliar zodiacs of broken light
Sweep a dark glass of stained windows,
Where reflected figures are not our own.

Trapped in carved garden fountains,
Lovers embrace a set of empty years.

Your heaven is a dark evening
Filled with white plane trees and falling water -

Where I come to you in forgiveness of our ending youth.

Zeitlos
<Trevi>

Unfocused,
It was a white breath of voices and cascades -

A burnished red of the failing sun
        again coming across your turned face.
A blurred coma of passing silhouettes,
Where crowds blur to one in a finish of numberless days.

All lives and no lives –
All futures become final.
All pasts remain open.

And there was a faint homily of falling water
Smoothing cut stones
Under a remaining catastrophe of stars.